#36 Los Feliz Branch Library
1874 Hillhurst Avenue
Los Angeles, CA 90027

JUN 10 2019

CAREERS IN THE
BUILDING TRADES

Apprenticeships

Careers in the Building Trades

A Growing Demand

 Apprenticeships

 Carpenter

 Construction & Building Inspector

 Electrician

 Flooring Installer

 Heating and Cooling Technician

 Masonry Worker

 Plumber

 Roofer

 Working in Green Construction

CAREERS IN THE
BUILDING TRADES

A GROWING DEMAND

Apprenticeships

Laura D. Radley

MASON CREST

Mason Crest
450 Parkway Drive, Suite D
Broomall, Pennsylvania 19008
(866) MCP-BOOK (toll-free)
www.masoncrest.com

First printing

9 8 7 6 5 4 3 2 1

ISBN (hardback) 978-1-4222-4111-0
ISBN (series) 978-1-4222-4110-3
ISBN (ebook) 978-1-4222-7681-5

Cataloging-in-Publication Data on file with the Library of Congress

NATIONAL
HIGHLIGHTS

Developed and Produced by National Highlights Inc.
Editor: Andrew Morkes
Proofreader: Mika Jin
Interior and cover design: Yolanda Van Cooten
Production: Michelle Luke

QR CODES AND LINKS TO THIRD-PARTY CONTENT
You may gain access to certain third-party content ("Third-Party Sites") by scanning and using the QR Codes that appear in this publication (the "QR Codes"). We do not operate or control in any respect any information, products, or services on such Third-Party Sites linked to by us via the QR Codes included in this publication, and we assume no responsibility for any materials you may access using the QR Codes. Your use of the QR Codes may be subject to terms, limitations, or restrictions set forth in the applicable terms of use or otherwise established by the owners of the Third-Party Sites. Our linking to such Third-Party Sites via the QR Codes does not imply an endorsement or sponsorship of such Third-Party Sites or the information, products, or services offered on or through the Third-Party Sites, nor does it imply an endorsement or sponsorship of this publication by the owners of such Third-Party Sites.

CONTENTS

KEY ICONS TO LOOK FOR:

Words to understand: These words with their easy-to-understand definitions will increase the reader's understanding of the text while building vocabulary skills.

Sidebars: This boxed material within the main text allows readers to build knowledge, gain insights, explore possibilities, and broaden their perspectives by weaving together additional information to provide realistic and holistic perspectives.

Educational Videos: Readers can view videos by scanning our QR codes, providing them with additional educational content to supplement the text. Examples include news coverage, moments in history, speeches, iconic sports moments and much more!

Text-dependent questions: These questions send the reader back to the text for more careful attention to the evidence presented there.

Research projects: Readers are pointed toward areas of further inquiry connected to each chapter. Suggestions are provided for projects that encourage deeper research and analysis.

Series glossary of key terms: This back-of-the-book glossary contains terminology used throughout this series. Words found here increase the reader's ability to read and comprehend higher-level books and articles in this field.

INTRODUCTION

Apprenticeships have been around in some form or another for thousands of years, but, in recent years, they have become popular again. There are several reasons for this renewed popularity. Perhaps the most important reason is that they allow a person to learn valuable job skills without having to spend time and a lot of money on college or university studies. Young people can often join an apprenticeship program as soon as they graduate from high school. This allows them to earn money while they learn instead of taking out student loans to cover the cost of a good education. It's a good feeling to start your career without $50,000 to $200,000 in college loans. Additionally, many apprenticeship programs not only offer an hourly salary, but also benefits such as health insurance.

Those who complete apprenticeship programs often have better job opportunities than those who do not do so. In many cases the employer who provided the training is more than happy to hire an apprentice who is already familiar with company policy, procedures, and products. Those who do not receive a job offer from their apprenticeship employer usually have little trouble finding work because there is a shortage of trades workers in the United States and around the world. In fact, trades workers are the most in-demand occupational field in the Americas, Europe, the Middle East, and Africa, according to the human resource consulting firm ManpowerGroup. They ranked fourth in the Asia-Pacific region. The official certificate of graduation that an apprentice receives after completing an apprenticeship program shows employers that he or she has the skills and experience needed to do a job.

Apprenticeships also offer far more hands-on training than the average college or university program can provide. While classroom learning is an important part of any apprenticeship

program, an apprentice spends far more time on the job than the average college student. Additionally, the apprentice is often paired with several workers, giving him or her the opportunity to learn valuable skills from various experienced workers and instructors.

Apprenticeships are often the first step on a career ladder that can lead to amazing career success. Many apprentices have gone on to become successful business owners, sales executives, and educators. One reason apprentices do well later in life is that they learn not only industry-related skills, but also important soft skills such as the ability to work well with others, the ability to learn new skills on the go, a good work ethic, and the ability to come up with creative solutions for complex problems.

In summary, apprenticeship programs have a lot to offer anyone who wants a successful future. Read on to discover more about this amazing educational path and how participating in an apprenticeship can help you make your career dreams a reality.

Words to Understand

certificate: A credential that shows that a person has completed specialized education, passed a test, and met other requirements to qualify for work in a career or industry.

GED: An educational test that provides certification that is equivalent to a high school diploma for U.S. and Canadian students who did not complete high school.

journeyworker: A worker who has learned a trade and who can now be hired as a full-time professional. The traditional term for such a person is journeyman, but the terminology has changed because women now commonly participate in apprenticeship programs.

labor union: An organization of workers formed to advance its members' interests regarding wages, benefits, work conditions, and other employment-related issues.

probationary period: A period of testing and trial that a person must often undergo to determine if he or she is fit for a job or educational program.

CHAPTER 1

What Are Apprenticeships?

What Do Apprenticeships Entail?

An apprenticeship is an educational arrangement in which a person learns a skill, art, or job from an experienced, trained professional. The skilled worker teaches the apprentice skills, work habits, technical knowledge, safety practices, and problem-solving and teamwork strategies needed to become successful in that career. The person receiving training is known as an apprentice.

In the beginning, an apprentice is typically assigned simple, menial tasks. As the apprentice receives more training and experience, he or she is given new and increasingly challenging assignments to complete either alone or with supervision. In some instances, an apprentice may be rotated between various experienced workers to learn different facets of a trade.

■ An apprenticeship is a bit like an "industry scholarship." In fact, the training you receive could be worth up to $150,000. Above, an apprentice plumber works on a central heating boiler with her supervisor.

Classroom learning has been added as a component of modern apprenticeship programs to enable apprentices to learn skills and concepts that cannot be taught at a worksite.

The History of Apprenticeships

Apprenticeship programs have been around for thousands of years. It's likely that the builders of the pyramids in Egypt learned how to construct these stone masterpieces via an informal apprenticeship training program. Shipbuilders, doctors, scribes, teachers, farmers, merchants, and almost all other workers also learned their skills via apprenticeships. Even future rulers learned "on the go" as they were given more and more responsibilities with age. Apprenticeships for all trades and professions were common until modern times. In fact, lawyers, doctors, and dentists in the United States all learned their skills via apprenticeship until about one hundred years ago.

The Babylonian Code of Hammurabi is perhaps the first ancient text to outline clear laws governing apprenticeships. The code states that a teacher could not prevent an apprentice from returning home if the apprentice no longer wanted to continue learning from the teacher. On the other hand, it implies that students who were happy with the training provided by the master continued to work for the master for life. The relationship was viewed more as a father/son relationship than that of a teacher and student. The Greek philosophers Plato and Xenophon talked about apprenticeships in their written works, and ancient Roman writers talked about them as well.

In the past, an apprentice's teacher was typically called "master," and the relationship was far more involved than it is today. Masters were responsible for not only teaching a trade but also for ensuring that apprentices grew up to become fine young men who were honest, responsible, and hard working. In Colonial America, the law stated that masters had to be moral men who taught their apprentices to read and write and ensure that they received weekly religious instruction. Additionally, the state was responsible for supervising the apprentice until he or she reached the age of twenty-one or, in some cases, the age of twenty-four.

It's likely that informal apprentices helped construct the Great Pyramids of Egypt.

These classes are typically scheduled before or after work hours and may be held at a community college, at a vocational school, or even online.

Apprentices not only receive on-the-job training and experience, but they are also paid for their work. New apprentices in the United States are typically paid about half of what a regular, full-time worker is paid. Earnings increase as the apprentice gains experience. Advanced apprentices who have nearly completed their training may be paid about 90 percent of what an experienced worker earns.

In the United States, most apprenticeship training programs last four years. During this time an apprentice must complete a total of 2,000 work hours and 144 formal class hours per year. Some apprenticeship programs only last one to three years, but some take as long as six years. A growing number of apprenticeship programs don't have specific hourly requirements. Instead of completing set requirements, an apprentice must pass competence standards established by employers. Apprentices who work well may finish an apprenticeship faster than those who have a hard time learning new skills.

■ *Learn about the benefits of training to be a carpenter via an apprenticeship program.*

The Benefits of Participating in an Apprenticeship

An apprenticeship is a bit like an "industry scholarship." In fact, the training you receive could be worth up to $150,000, according to the U.S. Department of Labor. This arrangement makes it easy to learn a new skill without having to spend tens or even hundreds of thousands of dollars on college.

Famous Apprentices

Many famous people started off as apprentices. World-famous fashion designers Stella McCartney and Steve McQueen both started their careers as apprentices. Stella McCartney is perhaps one of the best-known fashion designers in the world, while Steve McQueen dressed famous people such as Madonna, Kate Moss, and Prince Charles of England. Sir Ian McKellen, the actor who has played film characters such as Magneto and Gandalf, started his career as an apprentice with Belgrade Theatre in Coventry, England. Famous chefs Jamie Oliver and Gordon Ramsay began their careers working as apprentices in the catering industry. Now that they are successful chefs, they offer apprenticeship training programs of their own for up-and-coming chefs and caterers.

Apprentices receive more hands-on training than a college student does. Those who get a job that involves physical labor—working with tools and/or working with complicated machinery—will be able to put what they have learned in a book into practice in daily life. Furthermore, an experienced worker can teach a new worker tips and shortcuts that may not be taught in a formal learning environment.

Working as an apprentice also makes it easy to find a job when the training is over. In fact, many apprentices receive job offers from the company that provided the apprenticeship training program. This is a great situation for both the apprentice and the company. The apprentice already knows people in the company, is familiar with the job duties, and does not have to spend time and money looking for a job. The company gains a valuable employee who does not need extra training because he or she is already familiar with the company.

Not all apprenticeships lead to full-time jobs. However, apprentices who must look for work after their training is over have an advantage over students who do not have hands-on training. Many employers value on-the-job experience and are more likely to hire a worker who has completed an apprenticeship than someone who has no on-the-job experience.

The Five Best Apprenticeships

 The best apprenticeable jobs are ones that pay well, offer plenty of current job opportunities, and are expected to be in demand in the future. Here are the five best careers that are apprenticeable, according to industry experts:

1. Police patrol officers

2. Computer specialists

3. Electricians

4. Pipefitters

5. Plumbers

Apprenticeships in the United States

More than 150,000 employers in the U.S. offer apprenticeships in more than 1,000 types of careers, according to the U.S. Department of Labor. In most cases, a person who wants to become an apprentice must be at least eighteen years old. However, there are some non-hazardous apprenticeship opportunities open to sixteen- and seventeen-year-olds.

Apprentices must have a GED or high school diploma. If the job involves physical labor, they must pass a medical exam. Employers usually contact apprenticeship applicants to ask them to come in for a job interview and expect the apprentices to show enthusiasm and aptitude for the job in question. In some cases, it can take weeks, months, or even years to get into a competitive apprenticeship program. Employers typically award points to each applicant based on interview results, educational qualifications, and aptitude. Those who have previous on-the-job experience may be awarded extra points. The applicants with the most points are selected for apprenticeship training.

In the United States, most apprenticeship programs are registered with the U.S. Department of Labor. Employers that offer registered apprenticeships must meet

■ *In the United States, most apprenticeship programs are registered with the U.S. Department of Labor. Above, the Memphis Electrical Joint Apprenticeship Training Center in Bartlett, Tennessee.*

■ *The well-known fashion designer Stella McCartney began her career as a fashion apprentice.*

standards of fairness, safety, and training. The apprenticeships are then funded by apprenticeship committees comprised of employers, employer associations, **labor unions** and, in the case of military apprenticeships, a branch of the military. A person who completes an apprenticeship receives a **certificate** conferring **journeyworker** status. This certificate is recognized in all fifty states.

Apprenticeships in Other Countries

There are apprenticeship programs in many countries around the world. However, some nations have more developed apprenticeship programs than others. These include the United States, the United Kingdom, Germany, France, Canada, and Australia. Countries with less-developed programs include South Africa, Turkey, India, Indonesia, and Egypt.

In the United Kingdom, apprenticeships used to be viewed as a second-class alternative to completing higher education at a college or university. This is no longer the case. In fact, many schools now offer pre-apprenticeship programs so young people can gain the skills needed to successfully apply for an apprenticeship. In the United Kingdom, apprenticeships must last at least one year, but can be as long as five years. There are intermediate, advanced, higher, and degree apprenticeship levels. Degree apprenticeships are on the same level as receiving a bachelor's or master's degree. The minimum age for applying for an apprenticeship is sixteen.

In the morning, my alarm goes off at 6am. I'll get out of bed, get dressed,

■ *Watch a day in the life of junior scientist apprentices at the National Physical Laboratory in the United Kingdom.*

Germany, which is considered to have the best apprenticeship training in the world, offers more than 330 apprenticeships in various areas. Apprentices receive on-the-job and technical training for two to three-and-a-half years and then complete an exam to finish their training. Apprentices who pass the exam are then able to find jobs not only in Germany, but in other European Union countries. (The European Union is a political and economic union of nearly thirty member countries.)

In Australia, apprenticeships are open to anyone of working age. These programs are also called *traineeships,* and you do not need any educational qualifications to sign up for one. In fact, you can even start an apprenticeship while studying in eleventh grade (the equivalent of junior year of high school in the United States). Companies can take on apprentices for a **probationary period** before beginning an actual apprenticeship. Once an apprentice is hired, he or she has the same rights as part- and full-time workers. Apprentices in Australia are entitled to leave (time away from the job for personal issues); allowances for buying tools, job-related travel, and/or buying a uniform; and paid time off to take courses related to the apprenticeship.

■ *Watch a day in the life of an apprentice plumber in Australia.*

In India, there are four types of apprenticeships. These are trade apprenticeships, graduate apprenticeships, technician apprenticeships, and technician (vocational) apprenticeships. An apprenticeship training period lasts anywhere from six months to four years. After an apprentice has completed training, he or she must take the All India Trade Test, an assessment exam that is administered by the National Council for Vocational Training. There are also laws governing what type of training an apprentice must receive, as well as how much he or she should be paid each month.

■ *In the United States, about 60 percent of all apprenticeships are in the construction industry.*

■ *The career of electrician is often listed amongst the best apprenticeable jobs.*

While each country has its own unique rules, requirements, and standards for apprentices, there are some similarities. Countries all over the world are looking for ways to harmonize (make the same or similar) apprenticeship programs across their own state or provincial borders so that the requirements and certificates received are similar across the country. Apprenticeships are becoming more popular around the world, and a growing number of employers are providing targeted training to meet the needs of women, ethnic minorities, and unemployed young people. Additionally, jobs that did not have apprenticeship training programs before now offer such programs.

Types of Apprenticeships

In the United States, about 60 percent of all apprenticeships are in the construction industry. Apprenticeship job opportunities in this industry include working as a welder, electrician, carpenter, pipefitter, plumber, or heating, ventilation, air-conditioning, and refrigeration technician, among other careers. However, plenty of other industries offer apprenticeship training programs. These include the biotechnology, energy, financial services, beauty, geospatial, manufacturing, information technology, health care, service/retail, and transportation industries. Police patrol officers, firefighters, fire inspectors, and dispatchers can also learn their trades through apprenticeship training programs.

The U.S. government offers plenty of apprenticeship opportunities. Federal government agencies that offer apprenticeship training programs include the U.S. Departments of Health and Human Services, Labor, and Treasury, and the U.S. Government Publishing Office. The United Services Military Apprenticeship Program is open to active duty Coast Guard, Marine Corps, and Navy service members. It provides members with the training needed to get a job upon reentering civilian life. A certificate is awarded at the end of the training program so apprentices will be at the same level as someone who has completed the same training in a civilian setting.

There are many factors that you will need to consider before applying for an apprenticeship. Make sure that you meet all the requirements for the job, because job requirements vary depending on your target position. Think about how many job openings there are in the field you want to study because newer apprenticeship opportunities may offer more and better future job opportunities than older ones that involve learning a trade that may become obsolete in the future. Think about your talents, abilities, and passions because you will learn much more from an apprenticeship that you are passionate about than one you are not truly interested in. It is also wise to consider the future salary and benefits offered by a career that you prepare for via an apprenticeship. Money is not everything, but you should try to work in a job that allows you to live comfortably. Taking time to choose an apprenticeship carefully will put you on the path to career success.

■ *An apprentice programs a computer numerical control system.*

Text-Dependent Questions

1. How can an aspiring apprentice earn "points" in order to increase his or her chances of getting into an apprenticeship program?

2. What country is said to have the best apprenticeship program in the world?

3. What famous people started their careers as apprentices?

Research Project

The U.S. Department of Labor offers a list of twelve top apprenticeship jobs at https://www.doleta.gov/oa/apprentices.cfm. Choose one and write about what it would be like to be an apprentice in this career.

CHAPTER 2

Apprenticeship Terms

apprentice: An individual who is employed to learn an apprenticeable occupation.

apprenticeable occupation: A skilled trade(s) or craft(s) profession that requires special skills and abilities.

apprenticeship agreement: A written agreement between an employer and an apprentice that establishes the terms of apprenticeship.

apprenticeship committee: An entity that provides apprenticeship and training services for employers and employees.

apprenticeship program: A plan for fully administering an apprenticeship agreement. This plan includes terms and conditions for the selection of apprentices, as well as a plan for providing hands-on and classroom training.

certificate of completion: An award, certificate, or diploma that proves that an apprentice has successfully completed his or her term of apprenticeship.

collective bargaining agreement: An agreement that is negotiated between a group of workers and an employer regarding salaries, benefits, working conditions, etc.

employer: A person or entity that employs an apprentice.

industry-wide standards: Current laws and regulations stipulating acceptable trade practices and the use of technological advances in certain trades.

joint: Indicates a program or agreement that is sponsored and/or managed by both an employer and a labor organization.

journeyworker: An individual who has the skills and certificate needed to be fully qualified to perform the work of a trade, craft, or occupation.

non-joint training program: An apprenticeship training program that does not include a collective bargaining agreement or the participation of a labor organization.

on-the-job training: Tasks learned while working. An apprentice in the United States must complete about 2,000 hours of on-the-job training tasks every year and show proficiency in these to graduate from the apprenticeship training program.

on-the-job training program: An apprenticeship training program that may last up to twenty-four months, but that does not include a related technical instruction component.

prevailing wage: Wages paid to the majority of trade workers in a specific area. The term "prevailing wage" usually denotes an hourly wage and is also used to determine overtime pay.

probation, disciplinary: Disciplinary probation denotes a time period when an apprentice is disciplined for failing to make satisfactory progress and/or for breaking company rules. During this time, an employer may withhold periodic wage increases, suspend part of the apprenticeship agreement, or even cancel the agreement altogether.

probation, initial: Initial probation is a time period immediately following an apprentice's acceptance into an apprenticeship program. During initial probation, an apprentice may need to follow additional rules and/or forgo certain rights given to regular apprentices.

proficiency: Mastery of a specific behavior or skill demonstrated by consistently superior performance, measured against established or popular standards.

related instruction: Classroom learning that reinforces on-the-job training. This instruction is provided either during working or non-working hours. Apprentices must complete 180 hours of related instruction every year.

supervision: The education, assistance, and control provided by one or more journey-level employers. Those who are officially providing supervision for an apprenticeship program must be on the job site with the apprentice(s) at least 75 percent of each working day.

suspension: To stop an apprentice temporarily from working. Suspension indicates that the apprenticeship agreement is temporarily void.

trade: Any job that has been defined by the U.S. Department of Labor's Office of Apprenticeships as being an apprenticeable occupation. Other countries have similar departments that classify apprenticeable occupations.

CHAPTER 3

Interviews with an Apprenticeship Instructor and Apprentices

Jeffry Lohr is the owner of JD Lohr Woodworking Studio and JD Lohr School of Woodworking in Schwenksville, Pennsylvania.

Q. Can you tell me about your background in the trades?

A. I founded Lohr Woodworking Studio in 1988 shortly after leaving my fourteen-year career as a high school shop teacher. I began by producing mostly reproduction pieces but, by 1994, I also had a huge portfolio of arts- and crafts-inspired original designs. However, because I was trained as a traditional industrial arts shop teacher and have a teaching background, mixing teaching with my regular furniture studio work was always part of my plan. In 2001, I opened the JD Lohr School of Woodworking, which is now an internationally-recognized destination for students from all over the world. I took on my first apprentice in 2006, and two of them are now not only journeyworkers, but also partial owners of the woodworking studio.

Q. Can you tell me a little about your apprenticeship program?

A. The apprenticeship I've run is a paid position that requires a two-year commitment from the applicant, of which the applicant is on a trial basis for the first ninety days. In total, it requires approximately four years to have enough experience to be classified at the lower master level.

also run a woodworking school one week out of each month. The apprentice takes my Practical Woodworking six-day intensive course during his or her first week of employment. In this course, the apprentice learns basic machining and safety procedures. This is then followed by actual shop work performing whatever tasks need to be done within the normal stream of our daily shop work. This can be anything from assisting in the sawmill, basic fabrication of easily-made parts on a cut list, sanding, or cleaning out the dust collector.

Although paid, the position is a minimum wage position because I/we are truly teaching each apprentice the trade. All aspects are covered—from drafting, illustration, and modeling to actual client presentation and drawing up a custom commission contract. All our work is done by contract because Lohr Woodworking Studio is a one-off type shop. This means each project is unique, and we do limited line production (or duplicate work) in our shop.

Apprentices move on from the initial stages of apprenticeship after four to eight months, or as soon as I am confident the apprentice can be trusted to be safe using all equipment and machinery in the shop. When this occurs, they are given permission and in fact encouraged to work on their own projects after hours. This is a free opportunity for the apprentice to develop his or her own creative voice. If any apprentice shows little to no ambition to grow and develop their own design sense and methodology by taking advantage of the free after-hours availability of the shop, equipment, materials, and tooling given freely to them, it's clear the individual will never really add anything to the business and I do not consider them someone I would want to keep as a full-time employee. After the required two-year period, the apprentice will be either given a significant livable wage or shown the door.

We only take on a new apprentice when we have enough work contracted over the months and years to come to support their wage and cost to us in providing their training. At this moment, JD Lohr Woodworking, Inc. is not currently in need of any additional apprentices.

Q. What advice would you give to young people who are contemplating a career in woodworking?

A. You should only go into fine woodworking because you are truly drawn to it and cannot imagine doing anything else. It is a love of the material and a fascination with process and design that will keep you in the trade and provide a reasonable living to you. You are mistaken if you think you will ever make six figures in the fine woodworking trade. That said, there is more currency to life than money. I never wake up in the morning where I am not excited to go to work out in the shop doing what I want to do—and enjoying every minute of it.

Andy Holloway is a diesel mechanic apprentice in the Michigan Caterpillar Think Big Program.

Q. What made you want to pursue an apprenticeship?

A. My father and other family members have worked in mechanics, construction, and other similar fields. That's always stuck with me. I like working on big equipment and fixing and testing out things. It's fun and interesting to see how it all works together. I enjoy working with my hands, and this job lets me do that.

Q. Was there anything about your apprenticeship that surprised you?

A. Not really. I knew what to expect from experiences that others in my family had. I completed one year of heavy automotive study and one year of heavy equipment study before this. I had also worked in a shop before, so I knew what I was getting into.

Q. What are the most important qualities for apprentices?

A. You have to be hardworking, show up on time, and not be afraid to get your hands dirty. You have to get in there and figure things out and ask questions if you don't know something. You must be positive and just keep going. You have to be responsible because you're working with expensive equipment—so you need to make the right decisions about what you are going to do.

Q. What are some of the pros and cons of being an apprentice?

A. Our semesters are divided in half, which means that half of the time we are working on the job and the other half of the time we are in school. There are two months that I am not working because I am taking classes and the classroom learning is in another state. So, I'm away from my family during this time. There is also a lot of manual labor involved and you must be willing to do it, and not everyone is. Sometimes it's rewarding, and sometimes it's just another day. Some days we work for up to twelve hours, depending on how much work there is and what department we are working in.

On the other hand, what I learn in the lab I apply back at the dealer. I'm getting training and experience on what I will actually work on in the future. When I am finished with my apprenticeship, I will become a full-time technician with Michigan Caterpillar and I will have an associate of applied science in diesel technology degree. Plus, the job pays very well.

Q. What advice would you give to young people who are considering a career in mechanics?

A. Stay positive. You must work hard and know what you are getting into because there are a lot of things that go into these machines and it's a lot of work.

Kahla Lichti completed an electrical apprenticeship and is now a certified electrician in Canada.

Q. What made you want to pursue an apprenticeship in electrical work? Was there anything about your apprenticeship that surprised you?

A. I pursued electrical work because I wanted to learn more about electricity. I was surprised by the mundane tasks and the way construction sites function.

Q. What's life like as an apprentice?

A. Life as an apprentice is essentially task driven and trying to be busy all the time. You are the lowest paid worker and are expected to be busy all the time doing something.

Q. What are the most important qualities for apprentices?

A. Listen, think ahead, ask questions, be early to work, wear appropriate attire, do not be hung over, bring sufficient food and water.

Q. What advice would you give to young people who are considering a career in electrical work?

A. It could be for you, or it could not, but you'll never know until you try.

■ *Apprenticeships are available in a wide range of fields, including woodworking.*

Words to Understand

blueprint reading: A class that teaches students how to read a design plan or technical drawing.

hazardous work: Work that is especially dangerous, and in which workers have a higher risk of injury or even death.

job interview: A formal discussion between a hiring manager and a job applicant. The hiring manager uses the interview to determine if the applicant is a good fit for the job.

reasonable job accommodations: A change or an adjustment offered by an employer to help an employee who has a disability do his or her job. Examples include making training or work facilities more accessible; modifying work schedules; or purchasing or modifying equipment, machinery, or tools.

CHAPTER 4

Learning More About and Applying for an Apprenticeship

How to Learn More About Apprenticeships

There are literally hundreds of types of apprenticeships, so it's important to learn as much as you can about them while you are still in school. Construction companies, energy companies, and employers in other industries that rely on technical workers likely have apprenticeship programs. Additionally, apprenticeships are rapidly expanding to many other fields. Some of the many industries that offer apprenticeship training include the engineering, information technology, restaurant, hotel, landscaping, insurance, pharmacy, and even health care sectors. Here are some ways to learn about apprenticeships.

Participate in Career Days

A career day is a day in school during which students learn about different career opportunities and educational training paths. A representative from an apprenticeship program will come to your school to provide more information about apprentice-

■ *Touring a construction site is a great way to learn more about the work of apprentices and trades workers.*

■ *Your high school teachers can help you learn more about apprenticeships.*

ships. At other career days, workers from specific careers—such as plumbers or bank tellers—visit to discuss their careers and what it takes to be successful. Career days also give apprenticeship directors and employers the opportunity to meet potential apprentices and employees. Ask your school counselor or shop teacher to set up a career day that focuses on apprenticeships and/or career opportunities in the trades or other areas in which you are interested. You should also consider touring a construction site to learn about potential career paths and the work environment.

Attend Open House Events

Some apprenticeship programs offer open houses on weeknights or weekends. These events include a tour of the training facility, a presentation by the apprenticeship director, an opportunity to try out tools and equipment, and a time to ask the director and apprentices questions about the program.

Visit Websites

The internet is a great source of information on any topic. However, it can also be easy to get lost if you don't know what you are looking for. Here are some types of websites you may want to look for to learn more about apprenticeships in general or to find out more about specific apprenticeships:

Community college websites: Many community colleges provide classroom learning opportunities for apprenticeship training programs.

Local trade union or apprenticeship organizations: Websites for these organizations can provide detailed information about apprenticeship program requirements and openings.

Local newspapers and magazines: Local news websites can help you discover upcoming apprenticeship-related events and opportunities in your local area.

State and federal government websites: Local and federal departments of labor offer great information on apprenticeship training that you won't want to miss out on.

Performing a keyword search using terms such as "apprenticeship programs," "government apprenticeships," and "how do I become an apprentice," will help you find good information. Don't forget to check out the list of websites at the end of this book.

Read Books

Library books are a great source of information on apprenticeships. You can borrow books about a particular trade if you already know what field you are interested in. Alternatively, you can use books to learn about various trades to see which ones are a good match for your skills, personality, and interests. Many free books, magazines, and flyers about apprenticeships are available online. Be sure to also check out the resources at the end of this book.

■ *Learn fifteen things that journeyworkers want to see in apprentices.*

Talk to Family, Friends, Career Counselors, and Teachers

Talking to people face-to-face is a great way to learn more about apprenticeships. If someone in your family completed or is working in an apprenticeship program, ask him or her what the work and pay are like, what the job requirements are, the pros and cons of working in a particular field, etc. You can also ask friends to give referrals to people they know who are familiar with apprenticeship training.

Career counselors and shop teachers at your school can provide invaluable help and advice that will help you learn more about apprenticeships. They can also help you identify your strengths and weaknesses, so you know what type of apprenticeship would be a good fit.

Also consider participating in an information interview with an apprenticeship coordinator or apprentice. An information interview is not like a **job interview**, where you must impress a hiring manager to be considered for a job. In this type of interview, you just gather information. You can conduct an information interview on the phone or in person. Ask your shop teacher or counselor to help arrange an interview.

Visit Military Recruitment Offices

Military recruitment offices may seem like a surprising source of information on apprenticeships. However, the U.S. military offers apprenticeship opportunities that are only available to active military members, the Reserves, and National Guard members. Helmets to Hardhats (https://www.helmetstohardhats.org), for

Four Ways to Make Your Cover Letter Stand Out

1. Start by stating the apprenticeship opening for which you are applying.

2. Discuss your strengths that would make you a good fit for the program.

3. List key skills you have for the position.

4. Tell about any related experience you have. This includes high school training, part-time jobs that helped you to develop applicable skills, experience with tools or equipment, etc.

example, connects U.S. military members with three- to five-year apprenticeship training programs in their area. All apprenticeship programs working with Helmets to Hardhats are federally approved, which means that military members who sign up for these programs are eligible to continue receiving G.I. Bill benefits.

What it Takes to be Eligible for an Apprenticeship

Entry-level requirements for an apprenticeship vary depending on where you live, what type of trade you want to learn, and even which employer you choose. However, the following general requirements apply to most apprenticeship jobs throughout the United States. If you live in a different country, contact your country's department of labor or apprenticeships for more information.

Minimum Age

In most cases, you will need to be at least eighteen years old to apply for an apprenticeship. This is particularly true if the apprenticeship involves hazardous work. However, there are a number of non-hazardous apprenticeship opportunities available to individuals from sixteen years on up or, in some cases, from seventeen years on up.

■ *Most apprenticeship programs require applicants to be at least eighteen years old because they sometimes involve hazardous work (such as risk of burns during welding).*

Educational Requirements

In most cases apprenticeship applicants are required to have either a high school diploma or a GED (in the U.S. and Canada). However, some programs are open to those who have not completed high school. Cement and concrete worker apprenticeship programs, for example, may only require proof of a tenth-grade education.

It's normal to make mistakes. They help us to learn and become better people. However, making certain mistakes when you participate in an apprenticeship interview can ruin your chances of being accepted into the program. Here are some particularly deadly mistakes to avoid at all costs:

Criticizing Others: Employers don't like applicants who badmouth others. Avoid speaking negatively about your parents, past or current teachers or supervisors, or others you have worked with in the past.

Poor Body Language: Avoid rolling your eyes, tapping your fingers or feet nervously, or presenting other bad body language (slouching, not making eye contact, etc.) that sends a message that you are disinterested and/or don't respect the interviewer.

Bringing Food or Drink: Don't bring food or a drink to the interview. It looks bad; plus, spilling the drink all over your documents or the person interviewing you is beyond embarrassing.

Answering Your Phone: Turn off your phone when you go for an interview. If you forget and it rings, apologize, and turn it off without answering the call unless it is an emergency.

Lying: Don't lie during the interview. The coordinator will probably find out the truth anyway by looking at your social media profiles.

On the other hand, many apprenticeship programs require applicants to have more than just a high school diploma. In some instances, an applicant will need to show that he or she has taken related classes such as metalworking, general shop, algebra, or blueprint reading. An employer may also ask an applicant about his or her high school grades to determine if the applicant has the skills needed to excel in apprenticeship training.

Fitness and Aptitude Requirements

It is important to note that the Americans with Disabilities Act clearly states that employers cannot turn down job applicants who have disabilities who can do the required work if they are provided with **reasonable job accommodations**. This law not only applies to full-time workers, but also apprentices. However, many trade apprenticeships do have minimum fitness and aptitude requirements. Some construction apprenticeships may require that applicants do not have a fear of heights. Other requirements involve demonstrating fine motor coordination and/or being able to lift a certain amount of weight.

Residency Status

Some apprenticeship programs require applicants to be citizens of the country where the program is located, while others accept anyone who has legal permission to work in the country. There are still others that do not ask for proof of citizenship or residency status.

Ability to Drive

Many construction companies assign work crews to various locations. For this reason, construction apprentices are frequently required to show a driver's license and proof that they have access to a vehicle. At the same time, apprenticeships based in a single location may ask applicants if they are able to get to the worksite via personal or public transport if they don't have access to a car.

Drug Testing

Many apprenticeships require applicants to take a drug test to determine if they have used illegal drugs. Furthermore, apprenticeship programs often have a zero-tolerance policy for illegal drugs.

Application

Applicants to an apprenticeship program will need to send in a completed application by the deadline. Supporting documents must be submitted with the application as well. These may include academic information, as well as contact information for people who can vouch for the applicant's character and abilities.

Interview

Getting an apprenticeship is a competitive process. Many people want to enter programs because they offer free training, a salary while one learns, and the opportunity to work in a stable, well-paying career once they complete the program. As a result, applicants must be well-prepared during the interview to explain why they are interested in the apprenticeship program and the career. Employers will often explain

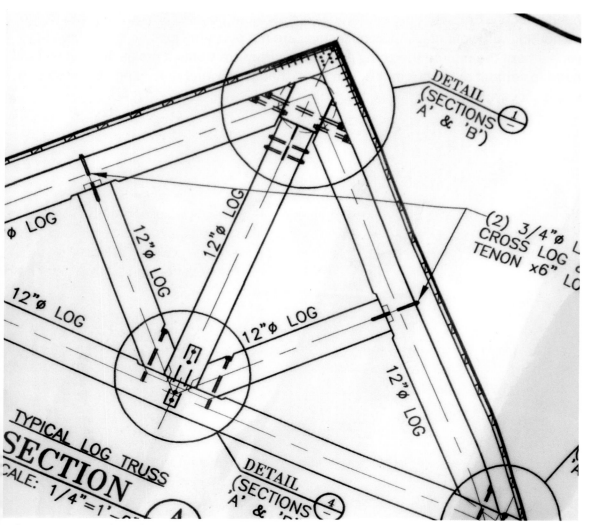

ø LOG

12"ø LOG

12"ø LOG

12"ø LOG

12"ø LOG

12"ø LOG

12"ø LOG

DETAIL
(SECTIONS
'A' & 'B')

(2) 3/4"ø L
CROSS LOG
TENON x6" LO

TYPICAL LOG TRUSS
SECTION
SCALE: 1/4"=1'

DETAIL
(SECTIONS
'A' &

■ *In some apprenticeship programs, applicants must be able to show that they have taken classes in blueprint reading.*

the challenges of an apprenticeship program to see if the applicant really wants the job. The applicant will need to show familiarity with the program and a desire to complete it at all costs.

How to Apply for an Apprenticeship

The first step in applying for an apprenticeship is to find one that is a good match for your skill set and interests. Don't apply for an apprenticeship just because you need a bit of extra spending money, or because your parents are pushing you to "do something with your life." Apprenticeships are not part-time jobs or internships that you can exit the minute the going gets tough. They are training programs that you will need to commit to long-term. Keep in mind that money and time is being invested in your success.

■ *It's important to make good eye contact and offer a firm handshake during an interview.*

Check the application deadline and requirements for the program. Begin filling out the application and gather the other paperwork you will need to submit ahead of time, so you can apply for the program before the application deadline. Be sure to not only submit required paperwork, but also other documents that can boost your chances of being accepted. A letter stating why you are interested in working in the trade in question shows that you are a serious candidate. This explanation will need to be adapted for every single apprenticeship program you apply for, so employers know that you are truly passionate about learning the skills they want to teach you. Try to also get a letter of recommendation from your shop teacher, school counselor, or someone else that you respect. Apprenticeship directors prefer applicants who come highly recommended.

Double check all your paperwork before you send it in. Make sure there are no grammar mistakes, spelling errors, or other issues in your application. Double check your contact information so that employers who are interested in your application can get in touch with you easily. Do the same if you included recommendations from your shop teacher, counselor, etc.

Prepare for an interview by purchasing suitable clothing. Most apprenticeship program coordinators won't expect you to show up in a suit and tie or a business outfit. However, you should be dressed in business casual wear. If you have tattoos on your arms or other body areas that are visible, you'll want to wear clothing that covers them. Women should avoid wearing gaudy jewelry and excess make-up.

Another important form of preparation is assessing your social media profile. It's estimated that more than 90 percent of all companies looking for people to hire visit applicants' social media websites to determine if a person is right for the job. A similar percentage of apprenticeship coordinators also probably review applicants' social media profiles. One reason employers/coordinators check a possible apprenticeship candidate's social media channels is to see if he or she has certain skills needed for success in the program. Apprenticeship coordinators are also looking for "red flags"—issues that will disqualify you from consideration. References to the use of illegal drugs, threats of violence, the use of profanity, inappropriate sexual posts, and evidence that an applicant drinks a lot of alcohol may lead a coordinator to disqualify you. Excessive spelling and/or grammar errors may make you lose points with the coordinator.

■ Apprenticeship coordinators often review applicants' social media profiles to be sure that everything that is posted online is positive and appropriate for all viewers.

If you have been turned down for a spot in an apprenticeship program in the past, don't pass up the opportunity to apply for it again if you are truly interested in the program. Many apprenticeships are competitive in nature and employers may turn you down simply because there is another candidate who has more experience, better grades, and/or has taken classes that you haven't taken. You can still successfully gain a spot in this apprenticeship program later if you improve your grades, take extra classes to boost your skills, or even do part-time work in a related field.

 ## Text-Dependent Questions

1. Where can you find more information about apprenticeships?

2. What are some requirements for applying for an apprenticeship?

3. What are some good classes to take to prepare for an apprenticeship?

 ## Research Project

Ask a friend to work with you on a mock interview. Pretend you have applied for an apprenticeship and you have been called in for an interview. Dress as you would for an interview and practice answering questions, talking about yourself, and explaining your skills and strengths. When you are finished, ask your friend to provide feedback on your performance.

■ *Apprentices participate in classroom learning at a community college.*

Words to Understand

component: A part of a larger plan, system, or product.

hybrid: Something that is created by combining two elements.

Occupational Safety and Health Administration: This agency was created by the U.S. Congress in 1970 to assure safe and healthy working conditions for employees by setting and enforcing standards and providing training, outreach, education, and assistance.

training model: A type or style of training.

CHAPTER 5

What to Expect from an Apprenticeship

It is important to realize that there really is no such thing as a "typical" apprenticeship. While many aspects of different apprenticeship programs are similar, there are differences between programs taught by different companies as well as obvious differences between different types of trade apprenticeships. Additionally, modern technology is changing every aspect of society, including apprenticeship programs. Employers and labor unions alike are continually adapting their ways of doing things to provide up-to-date apprenticeship training in the best way possible. Even so, the following information provides a detailed

■ *Roofing industry apprentices get hands-on experience at a job site.*

and accurate picture of what apprentices can expect from an apprenticeship training program.

Overview of a Typical Apprenticeship Program

Every apprenticeship training program in the United States has five main **components**.

1. **Business involvement:** Employers are closely involved in providing apprenticeship training. They work closely with program managers to ensure that training on current technologies and work practices is integrated into the program.

2. **Structured on-the-job training:** Apprentices are provided with step-by-step instructions for handling jobs. Work assignments start out simple and plenty of supervision is given to ensure that there are no mistakes or accidents. As an apprentice gains skill, he or she is given more challenging assignments to complete, and less supervision is required.

3. **Related instruction:** The apprentice participates in classroom learning that is typically provided by a local community college, vocational school, or technical school, not the employer.

4. **Rewards for skills gained:** An apprentice's salary gradually increases as he or she successfully learns new skills and obtains experience.

5. **Awarding of certificate:** A nationally recognized certificate is awarded to an apprentice who has successfully completed the training program. The certificate is accepted throughout the United States and shows that the apprentice has the skills and qualifications to take on full-time employment in his or her industry.

Training Models

Apprenticeship training programs can be time-based, competency-based, or use a **hybrid** approach. Time-based models require apprentices to complete a certain amount of on-the-job work, as well as study for a set number of hours. Competency-based programs allow apprentices to progress at their own pace. Apprentices in these programs take an exam to show if they are ready to graduate or need additional work or study time. Hybrid models combine elements of both time-based and competency-based apprenticeship programs. There is a minimum to maximum range of study and on-the-job training hours. Apprentices show competence by successfully demonstrating their skills at the end of the training course.

Most apprenticeship training programs combine related instruction with on-the-job training. However, there are also front-loaded programs in which apprentices must

■ *People who have a social personality type do well in apprenticeships that involve helping and interacting with people on a regular basis.*

complete a certain amount of related instruction before beginning on-the-job training. Segmented apprenticeships require apprentices to alternate between periods of related instruction and on-the-job training.

Some apprenticeship training programs have a pre-apprenticeship training segment built into the program so apprentices can learn basic skills needed to do basic jobs. In some instances, those who complete a pre-apprenticeship training program receive credit for having previous experience. One such program is available from the National Association of Home Builders (and its ancillary organization, the Home Builders Institute). The program is geared toward high school and college students, transitioning military members, veterans, justice-involved youth and adults, and unemployed and displaced workers. Programs are available in carpentry, building construction technology, weatherization, electrical, plumbing, landscaping, masonry, and painting.

What's Your Personality Type?

Career experts believe that there are six personality types. Your personality type plays a big role in your ability to be successful in a career. What type are you?

- **Realistic people** like working with machinery and/or tools, solving problems, and getting jobs done with little or no interaction with others.

- **Investigative people** enjoy working in jobs that require a lot of thinking. They are also likely to enjoy the classroom learning aspect of an apprenticeship program.

- **Artistic people** do well with trades that involve the use of patterns, forms, and creativity.

- **Social people** naturally do well in apprenticeships that involve helping and interacting with people on a regular basis.

- **Enterprising people** do well with jobs that involve making decisions and providing leadership.

- **Conventional people** enjoy working with data, following routines, and working in a structured environment.

■ *Female apprentices and journeymen plumbers and pipefitt[e]* *discuss the benefits o[f]* *working in the field, t[he]* *apprenticeship proces[s]* *and pre-apprenticeshi[p]* *programs.*

Apprenticeship Program Examples

Here are some examples of apprenticeship programs and what they offer to partici-
pants:

- The Dallas-area branch of **Habitat for Humanity** offers a two-year Habitat
Apprentice Training (HAT) program for those who are interested in a career in
the trades. The first year includes on-the-job and related training in lawn maintenance, landscaping, fence installation, framing, flatwork, roofing, sheetrocking,

You will need strong communication skills to be successful as an apprentice and in almost any career.

Pay and Benefits for Apprentices

Earnings for apprentices depend on many factors—such as where an apprentice lives, the program he or she works with, how many hours of overtime the apprentice puts in, the skill one is learning, and what stage of the apprenticeship program a person is at. However, the following statistics from PayScale.com detailing the average pay for apprentices will give you a general idea of what you'll earn:

- Apprentice carpenters: $15.53 an hour
- Apprentice electricians: $14.46 an hour
- Apprentice linemen: $18.81 an hour
- Apprentice plumbers: $13.38 an hour
- Apprentice sheet metal workers: $14.80 an hour
- Apprentice welders: $12.48 an hour

While some apprenticeships pay more than others, remember that a quality job offers more than just good pay. Look for jobs that offer additional benefits such as health insurance, dental insurance, vision insurance, and paid holidays. You may also want to look for programs that are located near your home and/or the educational institution where you are completing related learning. Being closer to home or the school you attend will save you time and money. Most of all, you want to find a career you love. Don't just look at the money. Choosing a trade or field that you are passionate about is the only way you will make it through years of challenging apprenticeship training.

and painting. The second year provides advanced and license skills training in project management, electrical repair, plumbing, and heating, ventilation, and air-conditioning. Unlike many other apprenticeship training programs, the HAT training programs also teaches apprentices financial literacy, conflict resolution, business etiquette skills, accountability, leadership, how to interact with law enforcement, and job search skills.

■ *Mistakes happen during training and on the job, and it's important to have a good sense of humor and not take yourself too seriously.*

- **Boeing** partners with the **International Association of Machinists & Aerospace Workers** to offer a jointly-managed apprenticeship training program. The program lasts four to five years and includes a probationary period at the start of each program. Apprentices may work first or second shift on a rotating schedule and are required to maintain a lesson-to-work hour ratio. Class instruction covers topics such as shop theory, algebra, geometry, trigonometry, compound angles, physics, composites, electronics, mechanics, metallurgy, and programming. On-the-job training is also provided.

- **Mike Holt Enterprises** provides training to apprentices who want to become electricians, contractors, inspectors, electrical engineers, or electrical instructors. Its apprenticeship training program lasts four years, and each year is divided into four quarters. There is a review and exam at the end of each of the first three quarters. At the end of the fourth quarter there is a final recap and a final exam. There are classes on Occupational Safety and Health Administration construction safety at the beginning of each year. First-year classes and on-the-job training involve learning basic electrical principles such as fundamentals of direct current, fundamentals of alternating current, and electrical theory. During their second year of training, apprentices learn about wiring methods and materials, as well as wiring protection. Third-year apprentices learn about equipment for general use, special equipment, and safety practices; they also receive training in solar technology. Fourth-year apprentices learn about estimating, code review, and National Electrical Code calculations, and receive leadership training.

- The **United Union of Roofers, Waterproofers and Allied Workers** offers an apprenticeship training program for roofers. The program lasts three-and-a-half years and provides on-the-job training during the day and classes in the evening. Apprentices learn about commercial and industrial roofing, single-ply roofing, modified bitumen roofing systems, how to protect roofing from ultraviolet rays and other environmental hazards, and other topics.

■ *Learn how a roofing apprentice developed social skills during his apprenticeship.*

Key Skills for Apprentices

There are many important skills that apprentices should have, but can't learn in a classroom or even on the job. Here are some of the most important traits:

Following safety rules during your training is extremely important. Above, an apprentice wears protective eyewear and gloves while working in a carpentry shop.

Communication Skills

Ironworkers, heavy machine operators, carpenters, welders, and most other trades workers need good communication skills and the ability to work well with people of all ages and from all walks of life. The ability to work as a member of a team isn't just about getting a job done quickly and properly; it can also be a matter of life and death. This is especially true on a construction site with heavy machinery and powerful tools.

Furthermore, apprentices who learn a skill that involves working with customers day in and day out will need to know how to interact with clients politely, honestly, and with confidence. They also need good listening skills. Medical industry apprentices must know how to interact with patients and their families. Apprentices in the hotel industry need to know how to interact with guests who may be upset, tired, or unable to speak English well. Strong communication skills will come in handy if a trades worker launches a business. They need effective communication and interpersonal skills to interact well with customers, coworkers, construction managers, and others.

A Good Sense of Humor

A good sense of humor is a must for any apprentice. It is all too easy to make a foolish (albeit not dangerous) mistake that leaves apprenticeship instructors and more advanced apprentices laughing. Don't take yourself too seriously. Remember, you are there to learn a trade, not to show off how much you already know.

Confidence

You need to have confidence in yourself, so you are not easily intimidated by instructors and/or other workers who may criticize your work in a less-than-polite manner. Self-confidence provides apprentices with the grit and fortitude needed to learn new skills quickly and complete their training. Furthermore, self-confidence enables you to see the long-term possibilities for the training you are receiving today. Confidence in your abilities will keep you from giving up or feeling "down." Many apprentices went from being lowly trainees to running large companies and earning six- or even seven-figure salaries. Others have become competent instructors in the trade. There is no reason for any apprentice to feel held back; anyone who is willing t work hard can make it in an apprenticeship.

Love of Challenges

Any trade involves plenty of challenges. Apprentices must be willing to look at challenges as learning opportunities and be willing to try new things on a regular basis. A positive attitude towards problems is also important.

A Respect for Safety Rules

Many trades can be dangerous if you disregard safety rules. A desire to follow safety rules will prevent accidents that could seriously injure you and/or your co-workers.

Text-Dependent Questions

1. What are the five components of every apprenticeship training program in the United States?

2. What are some popular apprenticeship training models?

3. Which skills do you need to have or develop to successfully complete an apprenticeship training program?

Research Project

Use the advice on learning about apprenticeships in your area to find a company that offers apprenticeship training programs. Write a report on the types of training methods it uses, what skills apprentices are expected to learn each year, and how much apprentices are paid at every stage of the apprenticeship.

■ *The American Hotel and Lodging Association recently announced that it was creating an apprenticeship program that offers a direct path to upper management.*

Words to Understand

discrimination: Treating people unjustly because of their race, age, religion, gender, skin color, and/or other factors.

emerging: Becoming known, visible, or prominent.

executive order: A rule or order issued by the president.

funding: Money provided, especially by an organization or government, for a purpose.

greywater recycling system: A water recovery system that re-uses greywater from showers, sinks, etc. for non-drinking purposes, such as for toilet flushing.

riveter: A person whose job it is to secure materials—often metal—together.

CHAPTER 6

Changing Perceptions of Apprenticeships

In the United States, apprenticeships have been generally viewed solely as a training course for those who wanted to enter a skilled trade or craft. This was an accurate perception until recently. In fact, only ten years ago most apprenticeship programs were only available in a handful of industries such as construction, building, mechanics, steamfitting, and childcare. However, this has changed drastically over the last decade.

The U.S. Department of Labor, other federal agencies, and a number of states made a push to expand apprenticeships to the health care industry, resulting in the creation of apprenticeship programs for forty health care occupations. Companies in other industries also began showing an interest in creating

■ *Unions, trade associations, and government agencies are working to encourage more young women to pursue apprenticeships.*

apprenticeship programs in other sectors, such as the geospatial industry, financial services industry, the information technology and networking industry, the telecom-

In 1639 a woman named Mary Arnold was sentenced to jail for refusing to stop brewing (making drinks such as beer and tea) as demanded by the male brewers of Westminster, England.

munications industry, and the public sector. The American Hotel and Lodging Association recently announced that it will create an apprenticeship program that offers a direct path to upper management. Hotel companies involved in the program include Hilton, Hyatt, Wyndham, and Stonebridge, and the program is expected to take on 2,250 apprentices over the next five years. New apprenticeable jobs in insurance and banking include underwriter support service worker, insurance claims adjuster, insurance underwriter, bank teller, banking underwriter, account reconciliation representative, and credit coordinator. Companies in this field that offer apprenticeship programs include Aon and Zurich.

■ View the stories of African-American women and men who are involved in apprenticeships in various construction trades.

Women in Apprenticeships

Apprenticeships are open to women of all ages and walks of life. Apprenticeable jobs include not only traditional "women's jobs" such as childcare and nursing, but also

Posters such as this were produced during World War II to encourage women to enter the workforce to help the war effort.

Getting to Know Rosie the Riveter

Rosie the **Riveter** isn't an actual person. She was a cultural icon representing women who worked in factories and shipyards while men joined the military to fight in World War II. This image of a powerful woman doing men's work was the inspiration for art, a song, and even a Hollywood movie. Millions of women responded to the call to help the war effort by learning construction work and other new trades. Unfortunately, the enthusiasm for women in the trades did not last long. Once the war ended, many factories laid off women to give jobs back to men who were returning from the war. While some women kept their jobs even after the war was over, most returned to traditional roles.

skilled trades such as carpentry, welding, electrical wiring, and heating, ventilation, and air-conditioning. A growing number of women are enrolling in the United Services Military Apprenticeship Program.

Unfortunately, this was not always the case. A few hundred years ago, most apprenticeships were only open to men. Women were offered some apprenticeable jobs, but only in certain fields such as the production of food, beverages, and clothing. Unfortunately, as trades became bigger and more profitable, men even forced women out of many of the trades they had been allowed to work in.

Times began changing in the 1960s when U.S. President Lyndon Johnson signed an **executive order** forbidding government contractors from discriminating against minorities such as African Americans, Native Americans, and Asian Americans. This order was later amended to specifically prohibit **discrimination** against women, as well. However, discrimination was still a problem in the trades industry until President Jimmy Carter signed an executive order in 1978 that set goals to include more women in construction trades. Additionally, the order made it clear that construction companies that did jobs for the U.S. government were responsible for treating women with respect as they worked, assigning two or more women to construction crews as much as possible, and providing work facilities that both men and women could use.

Apprenticeable jobs such as customer service representative are expected to be plentiful during the next decade.

International Trends and Forecasts for Apprenticeships

The United States is not the only country that is focusing on apprenticeships. Experts in the **United Kingdom** predict that, by 2050, most apprenticeship opportunities will be found in the management, health care, and social care sectors. They also predict that apprenticeship jobs in the IT and telecommunication industries will grow by 110 percent over the next thirty-five years, and that the country's economy will gain a whopping £100 billion through apprentice recruitment by 2050.

Elected officials in **Canada** are seeking ways to make it easy for apprentices to complete their technical training. The government's Flexibility and Innovation in Apprenticeship Technical Training pilot project is exploring the benefits of simulator training, e-learning modules, mobile classrooms, virtual classrooms, and flexible in-class training delivery approaches.

Experts in **Australia** have recently reported that apprenticeship programs are still very relevant in that country's economy. However, they also found that there are a lot of problems with its apprenticeship programs, including funding issues and confusing regulations. They predict these problems will persist unless the government acts to fix them.

Germany is facing current and future problems with its apprenticeship model to successfully train many young immigrants and refugees who have arrived in the country because of violence in the Middle East and other regions.

The U.S. government, state governments, women's unions and associations, and nonprofit organizations continue to play an important role in helping women obtain apprenticeships for high-paying jobs and in industries that are traditionally dominated by men. While many companies and organizations that provide apprenticeship

raining offer help to both men and women, some organizations are specifically
devoted to women apprentices. For example, Chicago Women in Trades (http://
chicagowomenintrades2.org) offers apprenticeship and pre-apprenticeship training
programs for women who want to learn welding or technical skills. Tradeswomen
Inc. (http://tradeswomen.org) is a California-based organization that is dedicated

*In recent years, apprenticeship programs have become available for computer numerically
controlled machine operators and other high-tech manufacturing workers.*

Doctors and Apprenticeships

Nearly all doctors participate in a program that is very similar to apprenticeship, although it is not officially called an apprenticeship training program. These programs are known as internships and residences and, like apprenticeships, combine on-the-job and classroom training to teach new doctors important skills. Doctors participating in a residency or internship program also receive a salary.

to recruiting more women into construction trades, helping women who begin trade apprenticeships to complete them, and boosting opportunities for women to learn leadership skills and progress in their careers.

Other well-known organizations dedicated specifically to women include:

- Non-Traditional Employment for Women (U.S., http://www.new-nyc.org)
- Utah Women in Trades (U.S., http://www.utahwomenintrades.org)
- Women Construction Owners & Executives (U.S., https://wcoeusa.org)
- National Association of Women in Construction (Australia, https://www.nawic.com.au)
- National Association of Women in Construction in the United Kingdom and Ireland (https://www.nawic.co.uk)
- Canadian Construction Women (https://www.constructionwomen.org)
- Canadian Association of Women in Construction (http://www.cawic.ca).

The U.S. Department of Labor (USDL) has a Women's Bureau (https://www.dol.gov/wb) that is specifically dedicated to promoting apprenticeships for women in the trades. The department recently awarded nearly $1.5 million in grants to support employers that successfully recruit, train, and keep women in skilled occupations. The money will be used by several organizations to create pre-apprenticeship and nontraditional training programs for women, teach employers and unions how to create a supportive work environment that enables women to become successful journeyworkers, and provide support groups for women to help them complete training.

Apprenticeship opportunities for women have grown considerably over the last decade. However, there is still a lot more room for growth. Only 6 percent of all apprentices in the United States are women, according to the USDL, even though almost half of all full-time employees in all fields are female.

■ *Learn more about Rosie the Riveter.*

How Will the Apprenticeship Model Change in the Future?

Apprenticeships are becoming more accepted in the United States as leaders from the Democratic and Republican parties encourage industries to develop apprenticeship training plans. In 2015, President Barack Obama awarded $175 million in apprenticeship grants. This was the first ever programmatic **funding** for registered apprenticeship in the United States. In 2017, President Donald Trump endorsed a plan to create five million apprenticeships in the next five years. He said he would set aside about $200 million to give employers, unions, and trades groups more flexibility to design apprenticeship training programs.

Jobs that traditionally offer apprenticeship training programs are expected to grow now and in the future, which means that apprenticeship training in these industries is likely to grow as well. Some apprenticeable job opportunities that don't require a high school diploma and are likely to be plentiful in the next few years include those in retail sales, home health care and personal care, order filling, and food service. Apprenticeable jobs that require a high school diploma and that are expected to be plentiful through 2026 include those in maintenance and repair work,

■ *Many companies are creating special apprenticeship programs that teach skills such as solar panel installation to meet strong industry demand.*

customer service, first-line supervisory positions in various industries, childcare, law enforcement, secretarial and administrative work, and billing.

However, apprenticeship opportunities are already expanding beyond traditional trades. They are expanding into high-growth, highly technical industries such as information technology, advanced manufacturing, and health care. Apprenticeable jobs in these industries include computer numerically controlled machine operator, precision machinist, and mechatronics technician. Information technology (IT) apprenticeships are available in fields such as project management, security, and IT generalist work.

In 2016, The Healthcare Workforce Consortium received more than $7 million from the U.S. Department of Labor for new apprenticeship training programs. The organization will begin funding apprenticeships in health informatics, health information management, health information technology, and other fields. Amazon is even getting on the bandwagon. The e-commerce giant announced in early 2017 that it was creating an apprenticeship training program for veterans that would hire up to 25,000 apprentices by 2021.

Green Apprenticeships

Green jobs are those that produce goods and/or provide services that either benefit the environment or conserve natural resources. They can also be jobs in which workers make their company's processes more environmentally friendly than they were before and/or use fewer natural resources than before.

Registered apprenticeship programs will likely be one of the main training methods for individuals who want to do environmentally friendly work. Many companies have created special apprenticeship programs that teach skills such as working with greywater recycling systems, installing solar panels and sprinkler fitter systems, assessing energy efficiency, and identifying green practices. Other companies have incorporated green job training into apprenticeship programs that have been up and running for some time, teaching apprentices in these programs how to incorporate green technology into their work.

Green apprenticeship opportunities are likely to grow as the green economy expands. Many young people are far more attracted to jobs that have a significant positive impact on the environment than other commonly apprenticeable careers.

Developments That Will Fuel or Hinder Growth in Apprenticeships

There are many trends and developments that will fuel or hinder growth in apprenticeships. Here is an overview of the most important trends:

The Job Market

Job market opportunities will have a big impact on apprenticeship growth and decline. The more jobs there are in an apprenticeable field, the more apprenticeship opportunities are likely to be available. If an industry declines, then apprenticeship opportunities in this industry will likely decline as well.

Funding

In the United States and other countries, companies rely on government funding to provide apprenticeship training. An increase in funding and grants will likely lead to increased apprenticeship growth in many fields. Luckily, there is support from both major political parties in the United States for apprenticeship training funding. However, there is no guarantee that funding will increase in the near future. There is also no guarantee that funding would not be withdrawn by a future administration.

Negative Outlooks

Some companies have reported that negative ideas about apprenticeships make it hard to find young people who are interested in learning a trade via on-the-job training. Parents and young people alike are likely to view college as being a better option than an apprenticeship, making it hard for companies offering apprenticeships to recruit college students. But studies show that only 35 percent of future jobs in the United States will require a four-year degree or higher. Employers are fighting back against negative mindsets by targeting students in high school and in some cases even as early as eighth grade.

Declining Union Membership

Historically, unions have played a very large role in offering apprenticeship programs. They help local employers create competency-based programs that ensure future journeyworkers have all the skills needed to be successful in their trade. They have also been effective in helping underrepresented groups (women and African-Amer-

Unions and trades associations are working hard to educate people about the excellent opportunities, good pay, and rewarding work environments that are available for those who complete apprenticeship programs.

icans and other minorities) to enter and perform well in apprenticeships. Unfortunately, union membership is declining, and this is hindering apprenticeship growth in the United States.

■ *Learn more about apprentice training for union carpenters.*

Expansion into Non-Traditional Industries

Apprenticeships need to increase in industries that do not usually train new workers in this manner. That is why the U.S. Department of Labor's Office of Apprenticeship has successfully pushed to register new apprenticeship programs in rapidly growing industries such as advanced manufacturing, health care, information technology, and biotechnology. The good news is that the Office of Apprenticeship has been successful in creating new types of apprenticeships in these fields. However, these new programs still only account for 30 percent of all active apprentices. The top ten occupations with the most apprentice workers are still construction specialties such as electrical work, plumbing, carpentry, sheet metal working, roofing, painting, and pipefitting.

Text-Dependent Questions

1. What are some industries that didn't offer apprenticeship training in the past, but that are now offering this type of training?

2. What are green jobs?

3. What are some developments that could either help or hinder apprenticeships?

Research Project

Check out the O*NET's list of new and **emerging** green jobs at https://www. onetcenter.org/green/emerging.html. Does a job on this list interest you? Are there jobs listed here that you haven't heard of before, but that sound interesting? Choose one job and write about it. Include not only the job description and an outline of how you could learn the job via an apprenticeship training program, but also what you think the job will be like in the future.

apprentice: A trainee who is enrolled in a program that prepares them to work as a skilled trades worker. Apprentices must complete 2,000 hours of on-the-job training and 144 hours of related classroom instruction during a four- to five-year course of study. They are paid a salary that increases as they obtain experience.

apprenticeship: A formal training program that often consists of 2,000 hours of on-the-job training and 144 hours of related classroom instruction per year for four to five years.

bid: A formal offer created by a contractor or trades worker that details the work that will be done, the amount the company or individual will charge, and the time frame in which the work will be completed.

blueprints: A reproduction of a technical plan for the construction of a home or other structure. Blueprints are created by licensed architects.

building codes: A series of rules established by local, state, regional, and national governments that ensure safe construction. The National Electrical Code, which was developed by the National Fire Protection Association, is an example of a building code in the United States.

building information modeling software: A computer application that uses a 3D model-based process that helps construction, architecture, and engineering professionals to more efficiently plan, design, build, and manage buildings and infra-structure.

building materials: Any naturally-occurring (clay, rocks, sand, wood, etc.) or human-made substances (steel, cement, etc.) that are used to construct buildings and other structures.

building permit: Written permission from a government entity that allows trades workers to construct, alter, or otherwise work at a construction site.

community college: A private or public two-year college that awards certificates and associate degrees.

general contractor: A licensed individual or company that accepts primary respon-sibility for work done at a construction site or in another setting.

green construction: The planning, design, construction, and operation of structures in an environmentally responsible manner. Green construction stresses energy and water efficiency, the use of eco-friendly construction materials (when possible), indoor environmental quality, and the structure's overall effects on its site or the larger community. Also known as **green building**.

inspection: The process of reviewing/examining ongoing or recently completed construction work to ensure that it has been completed per the applicable building codes. Construction and building inspectors are employed by government agencies and private companies that provide inspection services to potential purchasers of new construction or remodeled buildings.

job foreman: A journeyman (male or female) who manages a group of other journeymen and apprentices on a project.

journeyman: A trades worker who has completed an apprenticeship training. If licensed, he or she can work without direct supervision, but, for large projects, must work under permits issued to a master electrician.

Leadership in Energy and Environmental Design (LEED) certification: A third-party verification that remodeled or newly constructed buildings have met the highest criteria for water efficiency, energy efficiency, the use of eco-friendly materials and building practices, indoor environmental quality, and other criteria. LEED certification is the most popular green building rating system in the world.

master trades worker: A trades professional who has a minimum level of experience (usually at least three to four years as a licensed professional) and who has passed an examination. Master trades workers manage journeymen, trades workers, and apprentices.

prefabricated: The manufacture or fabrication of certain components of a structure (walls, electrical components, etc.) away from the construction site. Prefabricated products are brought to the construction site and joined with existing structures or components.

schematic diagram: An illustration of the components of a system that uses abstract, graphic symbols instead of realistic pictures or illustrations.

self-employment: Working for oneself as a small business owner, rather than for a corporation or other employer. Self-employed people are responsible for generating their own income, and they must provide their own fringe benefits (such as health insurance).

smart home technology: A system of interconnected devices that perform certain actions to save energy, time, and money.

technical college: A public or private college that offers two- or four-year programs in practical subjects, such as the trades, information technology, applied sciences, agriculture, and engineering.

union: An organization that seeks to gain better wages, benefits, and working conditions for its members. Also called a **labor union** or **trade union**.

zoning permit: A document issued by a government body that stipulates that the project in question meets existing zoning rules for a geographic area.

zoning rules: Restrictions established by government bodies as to what type of structure can be built in a certain area. For example, many cities have zoning rules that restrict the construction of factories in residential areas.

Index

Photo Credits

Further Reading & Internet Resources

Cantor, Jeffrey A. *21st-Century Apprenticeship: Best Practices for Building a World-Class Workforce.* Santa Barbara, Calif.: Praeger, 2015.

Dykstra, Alison. *Green Construction: An Introduction to a Changing Industry.* San Francisco: Kirshner Books, 2016.

Editors of College & Career Press. *Nontraditional Careers for Women and Men: More Than 30 Great Jobs for Women and Men With Apprenticeships Through PhDs.* Chicago: College & Career Press LLC, 2012.

Graves, Colleen, and Aaron Graves. *The Big Book of Makerspace Projects: Inspiring Makers to Experiment, Create, and Learn.* New York: McGraw-Hill Education, 2016.

Harvey, James Sidney. *Seven Success Skills for Apprentices and Skilled Trades Persons,* Victoria, B.C., Canada: FriesenPress, 2014.

Internet Resources

https://www.dol.gov/apprenticeship: The Office of Apprenticeship of the U.S. Department of Labor (USDL) provides information on apprenticeship opportunities in construction, advanced manufacturing, finance, hospitality, and other fields.

http://www.careersinconstruction.ca/en/careers/getting-started/apprenticeships: This website from BuildForce Canada provides information on apprenticeships, videos of apprentices in various careers, and information on job duties, training, and salaries for a variety of construction workers.

https://www.australianapprenticeships.gov.au: This website provides information on apprenticeships in Australia.

https://www.gov.uk/topic/further-education-skills/apprenticeships: This website provides information on apprenticeships in the United Kingdom.

https://www.mynextmove.org/find/apprenticeship: Visit this website for a list of apprenticeable careers in the United States.

https://doleta.gov/oa/preapp/resources.cfm: This USDL website provides a list of organizations that offer assistance and practical training for women apprentices.

https://www.bls.gov/ooh: The *Occupational Outlook Handbook* provides information on job duties, educational requirements (including apprenticeships), salaries, and the employment outlook for hundreds of careers in the United States.

https://www.dol.gov/apprenticeship/toolkit/toolkitfaq.htm: This USDL website provides answers to frequently asked questions about apprenticeships.

About the Author

Laura D. Radley is a former ESL teacher with a passion for writing about skilled trades, apprenticeships, and job possibilities for young people. She has written books, blog posts, and articles for trade schools, vocational schools, career websites, and business owners in the trade industry and is always fascinated to discover new career opportunities that don't require an investment of tens of thousands of dollars in a college or university education.

Video Credits

Chapter 1: Learn about the benefits of training to be a carpenter via an apprenticeship program: http://x-qr.net/1Fb6

Watch a day in the life of junior scientist apprentices at the National Physical Laboratory in the United Kingdom: http://x-qr.net/1HtP

Watch a day in the life of an apprentice plumber in Australia: http://x-qr.net/1CwV

Chapter 4: Learn fifteen things that journeyworkers want to see in apprentices: http://x-qr.net/1DcP

Chapter 5: Female apprentices and journeymen plumbers and pipefitters discuss the benefits of working in the field, the apprenticeship process, and pre-apprenticeship programs: http://x-qr.net/1GD2

Learn how a roofing apprentice developed social skills during his apprenticeship: http://x-qr.net/1EG5

Chapter 6: View the stories of African-American women and men who are involved in apprenticeships in various construction trades: http://x-qr.net/1Eow

Learn more about Rosie the Riveter: http://x-qr.net/1Eww

Learn more about apprentice training for union carpenters: http://x-qr.net/1DYe